AF843471

INTERVIEWS

How To Succeed

INTERVIEWS
How To Succeed

Roderic Ashley

TYNRON PRESS

© Roderic Ashley, 1990

First published in 1990 by
Tynron Press
Unit 3 Turnpike Close
Lutterworth
Leicestershire LE17 4JA
England

Reprinted 1992

ISBN 1-871948-74-6
All rights reserved

Cover design by Eric Yeo
Typeset in Singapore by Linographic Services Pte Ltd
Printed in Singapore by Chong Moh Offset (Pte) Ltd

CONTENTS

INTRODUCTION

This book consists of two parts. Part One is designed to help you towards getting that all-important job interview.The author shows the way a covering letter should be written to sell yourself successfully to the employer. Often we forget that employers are busy people who would rather read a letter that is short and to the point than a long winded one. It is also important to note that although an employer may not specify that you should submit a curriculum vitae or covering letter, he will actually discriminate against those who do not.

We often overlook the fact that the way the covering letter or CV is presented reflects your personality. Your letter speaks for you even before you can do so in person.

Part Two is designed to help you prepare for the interview. Gaining an interview is something to be proud of, not afraid of. What an employer is saying to you basically is: "We like the look of you on paper and you've made us interested enough to want to see you in the flesh." So, gaining an interview is a compliment, not a threat. Included in this section are pointers on answering difficult questions and presenting yourself in the best possible way.

PART ONE

STEP ONE

OBTAINING DETAILS OF THE JOB

Sources of Information

Job Centre or Employment Agency

If you see or are notified of a promising job in one of these places, the initial information about the job will be available there and then. So too should be information on how you should contact the employer for further information or an interview. Make the most of the services and facilities offered by such job agencies.

Newspaper Advertisement

Although a frequent source of information, they are often misused. Look at the following advertisement. You will note that there are two ways of obtaining the information.

Borough of Lliw Valley

HOUSING AND ENVIRONMENT DEPARTMENT

Applications are invited for the undermentioned vacancies

(a) **DISTRICT ENVIRONMENTAL HEALTH OFFICER**
Scale 6 s.o.1 £11,190–13,270 p.a.
Applicants for this post must possess the Diploma of the Environmental Health Officer's Education Board, or equivalent. The successful applicant can expect to participate in the full range of environmental health functions within the Borough.

(b) **ASSISTANT D.L.O. MANAGER**
Scale 6 £11,190–12,301 p.a.
This is a new post and the successful applicant will be required to assist the D.L.O. Manager to organise and motivate a small workforce in a competitive environment. Applicants must possess 3 G.C.E. 'O' Levels (Grade 'C' or above) including English Language and Mathematics, O.N.C. Building or equivalent. Extensive experience of building maintenance and construction in a supervisory capacity is also essential.

(c) **TECHNICAL ASSISTANT (Grants)**
Scale 5 £9,966–10,647 p.a.
The post holder will be required to perform varied duties relating to renovation grants in the private sector. Applicants must possess 3 G.C.E. 'O' Levels (Grade 'C' or above) including English Language and Mathematics, O.N.C. Building, or equivalent. Previous experience is also desirable.

(d) **RESIDENT CARETAKER/RELIEF WARDEN**
Scale 1 £4,452–7,621 p.a.
This post is a full-time residential appointment and the successful applicant will act as caretaker of a single person housing complex at Loughor, and as a relief warden at an adjacent sheltered housing complex. Rent free accommodation will be provided. No formal qualifications are required but applicants must be able to demonstrate a sympathetic and caring attitude.

For posts (a), (b) and (c) a car allowance is payable for official journeys.

Application forms and further particulars may be obtained from the Management Services Unit, Lliw Valley Borough Council, Civic Centre, Penilergaer, Swansea, SA4 1GH, Tel. Gorseinon 893081, Ext. 140.
Closing date 12 noon on the 6th August, 1990.

J.C. HOWELLS (Chief Executive)

By Letter

Even a letter requesting details may be used as "evidence" in assessing your suitability. Some organisations keep the detail requests and attach them to the other material submitted by short-listed candidates. So don't let yourself down at the outset by a scrappy letter.

Key Points:

* Keep the letter brief
* Keep the letter neat
* Specify the job/job reference you're interested in
* If you're asked to enclose an sae, do so, otherwise you may receive nothing. (N.B. Enclose a **large** envelope.)

Contrast the two letters below.

(a)

32 Bolton Road
Highwick
Brookside
NB2 6BF
14 June 199-

The Personnel Manager
Dankworth Mills
Brookside
NB4 7TP

Dear Sir

Would you please send me details of the post of **Clerical Assistant (Ref CA/2)**, advertised in today's 'Brookside Post'.

Yours faithfully

Madiha Hassan
MADIHA HASSAN (Mrs)

(b)

81 Church Tower
Lowick
Brookside

Dear Sir

Can you send me details of the job you've got vacant.

Yours
Bert Veale

Letter A is clear, polite, specific and neat. Letter B is vague, blunt and it is not clear who the letter is addressed to, let alone which job it refers to. You are not expected to type your preliminary letter but it should still be set out clearly. (N.B. Use the 'blocked' layout as in A.)

By Telephone

If you may phone for details, make sure that you have the following on hand before you start the call:

* the job title/reference
* where/when you saw the advertisement
* your address, including post code
* enough coins if using a payphone.

Your tone should be polite and your voice clear. Be confident, not apologetic. The company has invited you to phone.

STEP TWO

COMPLETING THE APPLICATION FORM

Not all jobs will require completed application forms. In particular, small employers find it hard to justify the expense of printed forms if they have only a few employees. They will, instead, rely more heavily on CVs and letters.

There is always a moment of excitement and lifted spirits when a job application form comes through the post. The great temptation is to fill it in immediately and rush down to the post box. ***DON'T***. It's the worst thing you can do. Personnel Officers will tell you that hastily completed forms are one of the principal reasons for rejecting applicants.

Instead, do the following:

Stage 1

Read through any accompanying information about the company and the job.

Note the closing date for applications.

Read through the application form carefully.

REFLECT: Do you want the job? A strange question perhaps in the current economic climate, but can you apply enthusiastically for a job which is not really for you? Your lack of enthusiasm will show through in your application, and will not help you to the short-list. Then, perhaps, that all too familiar depression will start again: why can't I get an interview?

Stage 2

Assuming that you do want the job, you will usually have at least a week before the applications are due in. Use that time to find out as much as you can about the company — its products, working conditions, labour relations etc. — from people you know who work there. It will help you prepare your application.

Meanwhile, consider the information requested in the form and find out in good time anything you need to, for example NI number, your weight etc.

(Application forms vary enormously in their design and layout. Remember that they are designed for the employer's benefit — to obtain the information he wants in the order that he wants it. They are not designed for the applicant's benefit, and there are some pretty awful forms which disadvantage the applicant. **This is a major reason why you should support your application with a CV and/or letter.)**

Stage 3

You may now think you are ready to complete your form. ***DON'T.*** Make a photocopy of the form and practise completing it.

You may find that you have to 'edit' certain information because of lack of space. It's better to find this out now.

Do the instructions say that you must complete in black ink, ballpoint pen or block capitals? If so, there is a special reason (like photocopying the form) and you ignore it at your peril!

It is always good practice to print in black ballpoint anyway.

There are sometimes problem areas on application forms which need to be sorted out before you start to write.

On the next page is a fairly standard sample application form. The more high-powered the job, the more complex the form is likely to be, but this one would cover a fairly wide range of job vacancies. Read through it and jot down any parts which might be problem areas for you.

POSITION APPLIED FOR:

XYZ COMPANY LTD

<table>
<tr><td colspan="2">SURNAME:</td><td colspan="2">FORENAMES:</td></tr>
<tr><td colspan="2">ADDRESS:</td><td colspan="2">TELEPHONE NO.:
HOME:
WORK:</td></tr>
<tr><td>AGE:</td><td>DATE OF
BIRTH:</td><td>PLACE OF
BIRTH:</td><td>MARITAL
STATUS:</td></tr>
<tr><td colspan="4">NUMBER AND AGE OF CHILDREN:</td></tr>
<tr><td colspan="4">EDUCATION AND TRAINING (secondary schools/colleges attended):</td></tr>
<tr><td colspan="4">QUALIFICATIONS (In chronological order):</td></tr>
<tr><td colspan="4">EXPERIENCE (In chronological order; include positions held and reasons for leaving):

(Use additional sheet if necessary) PTO</td></tr>
</table>

HEALTH (List any physical disability or serious illness):	PRESENT SALARY:

REFEREES (Give the names and addresses of two people, unrelated to you, from whom we can seek references):

1.

2.

WHEN COULD YOU START WORK?

YOU ARE INVITED TO GIVE ANY ADDITIONAL INFORMATION IN SUPPORT OF YOUR APPLICATION.

SIGNATURE:	DATE:

Problem Areas

There are three major areas of an application form where some people might have difficulties:

Qualifications

Sometimes the space allowed is absurdly small for someone with a lot of qualifications. Either print them in small letters or indicate that you have completed them fully on your CV.

On the other hand, some application forms have a large space for this section, which may prove an embarrassment for someone with moderate qualifications. Print in large letters to take up space and give full details of dates (eg. writing the month in full). **Don't** be tempted to include any exam failures just to take up space.

Experience

This can prove difficult for those seeking a first job. Always emphasise **any** experience gained in part-time employment, Saturday jobs, holiday jobs, voluntary work, or school or college work experience.

The employer is looking for experience here, not just past employment. So make the most of anything suitable, for example, being Treasurer of the local Angling Club will have given you experience of handling finances, book-keeping, working within budget, maybe having to submit a written report or give an oral summary of the accounts. What is vital is turning your past experience to your advantage. (N.B. See the section on this in the letter-writing unit.)

Open-Ended Questions

This is also dealt with fully in the section on the supporting letter, but briefly, this is an invitation by the employer to make yourself stand out from the run-of-the-mill applicant. It does not mean that unless you are an Olympic Gold Medallist you should leave it blank.

The employer is here looking at the **whole** person, not just a potential machine-operator, craftsman or sales representative.

Include any positions of responsibility held at work, school, college, voluntary or other organisations.

Include any sports or pastimes if there has been no relevant previous section.

Include any activity which shows you to be a responsible, mature or interesting person.

Other Points

Health: The employer may need to alert the applicant to some aspect of the job which may affect his/her health.

Marital Status: See CV section.

Referees: See CV section.

SUMMARY

1. Apply carefully for an application form.

2. Don't rush to complete the form. Read all the accompanying information and find out as much as you can about the company and the job.

3. When you are ready to apply, practise on a photocopy.

4. Decide any details which would be better expanded in a CV or letter.

5. Complete the real form, printing carefully in black ink.

6. Answer each section truthfully, but presenting yourself in the best light.

7. Complete all sections. Use n/a (not applicable) for any section that really does not apply (eg. maiden name for a man).

8. Keep your rough copy for reference.

STEP THREE

THE CURRICULUM VITAE

Curriculum Vitae (a Latin term which simply means 'the course of your life'), is often abbreviated to CV or called by another name — 'Career History' or 'Personal Information Sheet'.

An employer will frequently ask for a CV. If you have applied for jobs before, without writing your CV, you will find that composing one clarifies in your own mind your abilities and experience. You must decide which information is essential about you and what is unimportant for a prospective employer.

On the next sheet you will see a completed CV. Look at it briefly now to familiarise yourself with its structure. We will return to it later.

Structure of a Curriculum Vitae

A Curriculum Vitae should contain the following:

full name
address
telephone number(s)
date of birth
age
place of birth and nationality
marital status and details of any children
education (in chronological order)
qualifications obtained with dates and grades
professional bodies you belong to
employment outline
names of two referees with an accurate contact address
period of notice required from current job (if applicable)

There are several important points to note about these headings:

Each of the headings gives you a clear structure about what you should include or omit from each part of the CV.

Education

List only the secondary school(s) attended and any post-school education. Indicate whether this was full-time (f-t) or part-time (p-t).

Qualifications

Always give dates of qualifications and their exact title. Preparing this for a CV can avoid embarrassing attempts to remember dates or titles in an interview.

CURRICULUM VITAE

NAME:	Tina Gaynor Winston
ADDRESS:	17 Hilltop Heights, Belsize Park, Knebton, West Midlands. KN2 40P
TELEPHONE:	Home: 021 44 6572 Work: 021 67 3390 Ext. 402
DATE OF BIRTH:	17.09.68 **AGE:** 22
PLACE OF BIRTH:	Bridgetown, Barbados
NATIONALITY:	British
MARITAL STATUS:	Married No children
EDUCATION:	Chesterley Comprehensive School, Wigton 1979-1985 Wigton College of Further Education, 1985-1987 (f-t)
QUALIFICATIONS:	O level passes in English Language (B), Maths (C), Commerce (B), Geography (C), Art (C), (1985) BTEC National Certificate, Business Studies (1983) Basic Word Processing Course, Knebton College (day release, 10 days October 1990)
EXPERIENCE:	Clerical Officer, Finance Section, Knebton Borough Council, February 1989 to present. Clerical Assistant, Wages Department, Loamshire County Council, County Hall, Wigton, July 1987-January 1989
REFERENCES:	Mr J B Nixon Chief Clerical Officer Knebton Borough Council Town Hall High Street Knebton KN3 4JD Mrs J Hall Personnel Officer Loamshire County Council County Hall Wigton WIl 3BJ
PERIOD OF NOTICE:	One month

Remember that a mere list of qualifications will not necessarily impress an employer. The circumstances surrounding them will also contribute. An employer might look more favourably on the motivation of an applicant who has followed some City & Guilds courses in evening class than someone who took them as a full-time student.

Likewise, 10 'O' levels taken over a three-year period might not impress as much as 7 passed in a single attempt.

Don't forget to include any training qualifications from previous workplaces, the Forces, or voluntary organisations, eg. a First Aid Certificate from the St. John's Ambulance Brigade.

Note: Do **not** include any failures!

Marital Status

This means whether you are single, married, divorced, etc. Some people consider that this is being nosy — that their private life is none of an employer's business. Fair enough, but currently, it is an employer's market and there is no point in giving any grounds for rejecting your applications because of insufficient information. So make up your mind carefully on this point.

Remember that many employers are looking for a stable workforce — perhaps people with children and a mortgage who need that job to meet hefty outgoings. Family commitments would be seen here as a bonus, not a drawback — they might help you at the interview rather than hinder you.

Special Skills/Interests

This section is rather like the 'Tell us about yourself' section of the application form. Some people are often very reserved about announcing skills and abilities. Don't be. Be positive but not pushy. Try to convert your past experiences into positive bonuses.

For example, someone who is a keen footballer, applying for a security guard's job, will create the impression of being physically fit. Likewise, someone who likes orienteering, should be able to find their way around a large warehouse quickly if applying for a store supervisor's job.

References

Most employers will ask you to name two referees. The **referee** is the person you ask to give written confirmation of your abilities, honesty, initiative, suitability for the job etc. — the **reference** is what they write.

When choosing your referees, it is always preferable to include as one, your current or previous employer. If you are applying for a first job, use your last school headteacher or college principal. Even if you never spoke to your headteacher, use him or her, not your old form teacher with whom you happened to get on well. Rest assured that the head will always obtain information from people who knew you well before writing the reference.

For your other referee, choose someone whom you can trust to write fairly and convincingly about you, and preferably has a recognised position of authority in society.

List their full name and status (eg. GP; Minister of Religion; Councillor; Factory or Office Supervisor) **when** you have asked permission to use their name. Most people will be quite happy to help you, but won't be pleased if the first that they know of it is a reference request through the post.

Note: You **cannot** use a close relative as a referee.

When you do apply for a job, always inform your referees about the type of job, what it will involve, and why you think that you are suited to it. This will help them write a reference tailored specifically to that job.

GENERAL POINTS

Length of a CV

A friend, applying for jobs, once said: 'My CV is six sides long with all the experience I've had. I just don't know why I'm not getting interviews.'

He was not getting interviews **because** his CV was too long. He hadn't realised that an employer:

* uses a CV to help **summarise** a candidate's suitability and experience.

* values an employee's ability to summarise and select information. (My friend was demonstrating that he could not do this.)

* does not have time to read through masses of paper. (A six sheet CV will take 3 minutes to read through thoroughly. Just twenty applicants like this would mean an hour spent just to read the CVs!)

So, try to make your CV **no more than one sheet of A4** (the size of this paper).

If you really do need more space, keep your CV to a maximum of 2 sheets, and make sure that they are separate, numbered sheets with your name clearly at the top of the second sheet.

Typing Your CV

You **must** present a typed CV. Not only does it create a much better impression, it allows you to say more on a single sheet than larger handwriting will permit. If you can't type it yourself, ask someone who is a competent typist. If necessary, you can pay for it to be done — a stationer's or bookshop will probably be able to recommend a typist offering this service. It is not expensive, you will be impressed with the results (good for self-esteem) and it will save you a lot of problems later.

Ensure that you make several **photocopies** of the original CV and file them. If your application is unsuccessful this time, you can use these copies for future applications. But always photocopy this from the **original**, to avoid poor quality copies.

Take care, however, that the information is still accurate. In particular, check that:

* you are not older.
* you have not changed address.
* you have not gained further qualifications or training.
* that your referees are still appropriate for the job in question.

If necessary, update your CV — **never** send off an out-of-date one. (If you are lucky enough to have access to a word processor, updating is very easy. Again, you may find someone offering this service.)

Note how Tina Winston's completed CV on p.11 contained all the information relevant to supplement her application, without giving too much detail. The sheet is clear and uncluttered.

STEP FOUR

WRITING A LETTER OF APPLICATION

It is a normal practice to submit a letter of application together with a CV and the application form, if provided.

The reason for submitting a letter is straightforward.

> The application form allows the employer to see obvious differences in qualifications and background of the applicant, but on the employer's terms.
>
> The CV allows the applicant to expand on the above and 'highlight' aspects about himself/herself.
>
> The letter is the only means by which the applicant can show his/her own personality, motives and views because it is **created** by the applicant.

So the letter is arguably the most important aspect of the application, because it gives **you** the opportunity to **persuade** the employer to invite you to the interview.

Types of Letter

There are basically three types of letter:

* those contained within the application form.
* a covering letter.
* a full letter.

Which one you write will depend upon the other information you are required to submit. This is detailed below.

The Letter within an Application Form

Sometimes an application form will ask you to support your application by writing a letter on the final sheet of the form. You may be able to continue this letter on another sheet, but sometimes an employer limits the letter to just what will fit on the form.

Whichever applies, you will actually start your letter on the form. So, do **not** write your address at the top of the sheet. Since your letter is part of the form, it cannot go astray and you will waste valuable space by repeating information already on the form.

However, start your letter with a suitable greeting. (Details of greetings and endings are given later.)

If you are specifically told your letter must not go on to another sheet, you have to be very selective in your writing. Try not to repeat information contained elsewhere on the form or CV.

The Covering Letter

This is the most common kind of supporting letter. On a separate sheet of paper from your form and CV, you outline briefly why you are applying and highlight anything in your application you wish the employer to take special note of. Use phrases like — 'You will note that . . .' or 'As my CV mentions, I have had experience of . . .' Do this no more than twice though, in order to retain impact.

A covering letter should run to no more than one side of an A4 paper.

The Full Letter of Application

Look at the advertisement for the Kingsbridge Motor Company on p.19. 'Apply in writing together with your full CV' means 'Write a full letter of application'. Remember that this instruction is for a wide range of jobs.

There is no limit to the length of the full letter, although employers will not like long-winded letters. Remember that your CV pinpoints your experience and qualifications and that your letter should enhance this, not repeat it.

DO'S AND DON'TS OF LETTERS OF APPLICATION

Layout

Adopt the 'fully blocked' technique, which is now the most common in business and industry. This means that:

* the sections of the letter outside the main body are in blocks
* everything except your own address and the date is kept to the left margin
* there is no internal punctuation in the blocks except for capital letters
* paragraphs should have a one line gap between them
* start a new paragraph at the margin.

Madiha Hassan's letter on p.2 was an example of blocked layout.

The Inside Address

This address is identical to the one you write on the envelope. It is placed at the top left of the letter above the greeting and its function is to speed the letter to the recipient in large organisations where clerks open all the letters.

Example

Mrs P Burton
Personnel Director
Wayne's Department Store
40-44 Taylor Street
Blackthorpe
Lancashire
FY6 4TZ

Use the person's name and title if you know them both, otherwise use whichever one you do know.

Greeting

If you know the name of the person to whom you are writing, use it.

Dear Mrs Burton

If you know only the title, use 'Dear Sir' or 'Dear Madam'. You cannot tell from the above example whether the Personnel Manager is male or female. Unless Mrs Burton has the foresight to put her name in the information to applicants, she will have to accept being addressed as 'Sir'. **Don't** use 'Dear Sir/Madam' which is regarded as impersonal.

Ending

If you have greeted a person by name, use 'Yours sincerely'. If you greeted them by title, end 'Yours faithfully'. In either case, use a capital letter only for 'Yours'.

It is a good practice to print your name under your signature.

Turning Past Experiences into Positive Qualities

The letter invites you to talk briefly about yourself and to show what is special about you as an individual.

People who have had plenty of work experience may not feel that this is difficult for them to do. But remember that it applies equally to experiences outside work (membership of sports or voluntary bodies).

People who have been unemployed for some time, or even never been in paid employment, get rather nervous about this.

It's important here to think positively. Consider how you have developed skills through the experiences you've had. How, perhaps, an apparently trivial task has taught you something or proved that you have positive qualities.

Read through the following skills which a job applicant who has not been in paid employment for some years may consider herself to have:

Working within a budget	Socialising
Teacher	Entertaining
Psychologist/Therapist	Menu planning
Nurse	Working with machinery
Home improvements/interior design	Working with textiles
Time and motions expert	Co-ordinating activities
Planning/organising time	Culinary activities

What background do you think this applicant has? (Answer given in the next few lines below.)

The important skill is to turn potential negatives into positives.

Make a list **now** of your hobbies and interests.

What skills do they demand of you for you to be good at them? Make a list **now** to show positive qualities about yourself — qualities which you might want to bring out in a letter of application.

Answer: A housewife/mother.

Write or Type

Just as the employer likes the CV to be typed for clarity, so he likes the letter to be handwritten. It ties in with the letter expressing the personality of the writer. If your handwriting is appalling, then type the letter.

Other Points

Write on one side of the paper only.
Print your name at the top of any continuation sheets.
Number the sheets.

Examples

Let's look now at an imaginary covering letter in response to the following Kingsbridge advertisement for an experienced sales executive.

TRAINEE SALES EXECUTIVES

EXPERIENCED SALES EXECUTIVES

RECEPTIONISTS

CAR HIRE MANAGER

NIGHT WATCHPERSON

BODY SHOP MANAGER

SPRAYERS

PANEL BEATERS

STOREPERSON

OFFICE CLEANERS

TELE SALESPERSON

During the next few months the Kingsbridge Motor Company will be opening one of the country's most advanced Nissan centres in the Swansea Enterprise Zone. Consequently, we are recruiting the above personnel for what promises to be a highly successful new development.

We are looking for competent, enthusiastic applicants who are eager to succeed and prove their ability within a hardworking, busy environment.

All of these superb career opportunities offer good basic salaries, excellent working conditions and many other fringe benefits.

If you feel you qualify for any of the above vacancies please apply in writing to our Managing Director, Mr. R. Watson, at the address below, enclosing your full c.v. to date. All applications will be dealt with in total confidence.

Roy Watson's

NISSAN

KINGSBRIDGE

NISSAN

Motor Company Swansea

Swansea Road, Kingsbridge, Gorseinon, Swansea. (0792) 898631

49 St. David's Ave.
Rumney
Cardiff
S.Glam.

17th August 199-

Dear Sir

Please find enclosed my CV.

I've been a car salesman for ten years now, currently at IXL Motors, Bridgend.

I have recently been passed over for the job of Sales Manager and so wish to move on.

I have an excellent sales record and could do the same for your company.

I have a 2-litre Montego for my own use, BUPA and four weeks holiday. I would expect at least the same from you.

Please give me a week's notice for interview.

Yours

John Palmer

This letter has a number of faults. Before reading on, jot down what you think they are.

> 49 St. David's Ave. (1)
> Rumney
> Cardiff
> S.Glam. (2)
>
> 17th August 199-
>
> Dear Sir (3)
>
> (4)
>
> Please find enclosed my CV.
>
> (5) I've been a car salesman for ten years now, currently at IXL Motors, Bridgend.
>
> (6) I have recently been passed over for the job of Sales Manager and so wish to move on.
>
> (7) I have an excellent sales record and could do the same for your company.
>
> (8) I have a 2-litre Montego for my own use, BUPA and four weeks holiday. I would expect at least the same from you.
>
> (9) Please give me a week's notice for interview.
>
> Yours (10)
>
> John Palmer

The errors are:

1. Don't abbreviate any part of your address.
2. Include your postcode.
3. Always use an inside address, and greet the person by name if given.
4. Specify, before you begin, which job you're applying for in a multi-vacancy advertisement.
5. Use the same terminology as used in the advert — here 'sales executive' not 'car salesman'.

6. A fatal error. The applicant gives his real reason for applying — that he's been passed over for promotion. While it is a very real motive for applying for a new job, don't expose it. It sounds negative.

7. The tone is arrogant.

8. The applicant is dictating terms of employment before he's even been short-listed. Such matters are for **negotiation** at the interview.

9. Arrogant again. The applicant assumes he will get an interview.

10. No formal signing off or printed name.

Overall, this is a very poor letter, shrieking of an applicant with a big idea of himself, and an equally big chip on his shoulder. (Note how many of the sentences begin with an ego-boosting 'I'.) Even if he is a good salesman, he has thrown his chances away for this job.

Structure and tone of your letter

Read through the job description or other details provided about the job. From this, work out what qualities the employer is seeking. Note the qualities stated in the Kingsbridge advertisement:

> 'We are looking for competent, enthusiastic applicants who are eager to succeed and prove their ability within a hardworking, busy environment.'

Your letter should try to deal with each point of experience or personality that the job description requires — grouped into general categories.

So, if a job description says, 'An essential quality is the ability to work successfully in a team', **don't** write 'I am very good at teamwork'. Instead, express it as 'I enjoy the stimulus of working in a team. In my present position I lead the team dealing with Product X and learnt much about Marketing and Public Relations from this experience'.

Likewise, rather than saying 'I did . . .', say 'I was given the opportunity to do . . .' This conveys self-confidence without arrogance and implies that others had trust in you. Talk about 'managing people' or 'supervising people' rather than 'telling people what to do' etc.

Select your phrases thoughtfully, taking care at the same time to keep your language simple and straightforward. Start a new paragraph for each major new point and try to keep paragraph length to no more than five lines — ten at the most.

Avoid running down your current employer: criticism might suggest that it's **your** personality which is the problem. Avoid also, mentioning that you are attracted by increased pay: that is obvious and accepted as a contributory factor in your application. But to state it outright will give the impression that it is the over-riding reason for your application and make you seem superficial.

Above all, show how you think that **you** are suited to the requirements of the job. This also means 'highlighting' or selecting those experiences which are most appropriate to the job.

If appropriate, give your own views on the prospects offered by working for that organisation. For example,

> A teacher, applying for a job with a school opting out of local authority control, might say: 'I would welcome the opportunity of being involved in this major new development in education.'
>
> A clerical assistant, hoping to transfer from a traditional office to an electronic office, might write: 'I am enthusiastic about the prospect of working in a new, exciting environment.'
>
> A manual worker, hoping to join a Japanese manufacturer, might say: 'I am keen to join a go-ahead company with new management techniques which allow worker involvement in solving problems.'

Don't play **all** your cards in the letter of application. Your aim must be to arouse the interest and curiosity of the employer; to make him think 'This person sounds interesting — let's invite him/her along to interview'.

Close by offering the employer the chance to find out more about you at the interview — eg. 'Should you wish me to enlarge upon any of the above points, I should be delighted to do so at the interview.'

SUMMARY

1. Observe conventions of letter layout.

2. Sound confident, not pushy.

3. Keep your style simple.

4. Meet the demands of the job description point by point if you can.

5. Give a brief summary of how you think your experience/qualifications make you a suitable candidate.

6. Avoid negative statements.

7. Turn your past experiences to positive qualities.

8. Avoid showing that you are motivated by the pay.

9. Offer a tempting invitation to the employer to find out more about you at the interview.

SAMPLE LETTERS OF APPLICATION

See the advertisement on p.19 for experienced sales executives at Kingsbridge Motor Company.

Brief Letter on Application Form

With this example, there is no application form to complete. If there had been, with a small section for a 'letter', the following might have been written.

> Dear Mr Watson
>
> The details outlined in my curriculum vitae have given me wide experiences of sales with a busy Japanese franchise, where I specialised, over the last two years, in Fleet Sales.
>
> I would welcome the opportunity to extend my career with a larger franchise to which I could bring my experience.
>
> Yours sincerely
>
> John Roberts

The letter is very brief and to the point. However, it still mentions key words and phrases: 'busy Japanese franchise'; 'specialised'; 'career'; 'experience'. The writer has not printed his name because it is printed on the accompanying CV.

Covering Letter

18 Grafton Rise
Pelham
Blankshire
BL4 7JG
17th August 199-

Mr R Watson
Managing Director
Kingsbridge Motor Company
Swansea Road
Kingsbridge
Gorseinon
Swansea

Dear Mr Watson

Ref. Experienced Sales Executive

Please find attached my CV supporting my application for the above position.

For the last three years of my seven year career as a sales executive, I have been with the Blankshire Toyota dealership, BT Garages.

The annual sales figures have risen steadily to 250 plus vehicles. A significant increase came with the creation of a Fleet Sales section, which I was asked to head. This gave me valuable experience in dealing with business customers who require satisfaction, reliability and cost-effectiveness.

I was fortunate to attend a number of courses run by Toyota (GB) which gave me added insight into Japanese car manufacturers' sales techniques, and particularly in creating customer loyalty.

I wish to extend my career now and consider that a sales executive's post for the higher-volume Nissan vehicles would offer me a welcome challenge, whilst capitalising on the valuable experience gained.

Should you wish to call me to interview, I should be delighted to attend.

Yours sincerely

John Roberts

JOHN ROBERTS

Note: This letter indicates substantial experience (seven years) as a sales executive in a busy environment; it stresses the familiarity with Japanese techniques, the trust and leadership given to the candidate with regard to fleet sales, the drive and enthusiasm to work for a larger organisation, and the concept of giving customer satisfaction. The writer has successfully 'edited out' any information not of direct relevance on a covering letter.

Full Letter

18 Grafton Rise
Pelham
Blankshire
BL4 7JG
17th August 199-

Mr R Watson
Managing Director
Kingsbridge Motor Company
Swansea Road
Kingsbridge
Gorseinon
Swansea

Dear Mr Watson

Ref. Experienced Sales Executive

Please find attached my CV supporting my application for the above position.

I have worked in the motor trade for eight years, seven of these being on the sales side. Although my employment began as an assistant in the Parts Department of BT Garages Blankshire, I was invited to become a trainee sales executive when the garage switched to the Toyota franchise. I believe that my initial year's work gave me a good insight into the problems faced by customers after the initial sale, and I learnt a lot about customer satisfaction.

I received my sales training from the sales manager at BT, together with several courses (listed on my CV) from Toyota (GB).

Two years ago I was asked to co-ordinate the Fleet Sales at BT, which I found very stimulating. Dealing with corporate customers as well as private buyers taught me a lot about both marketing — as opposed to selling — and meeting the stringent requirements of the Fleet Sales sector.

Sales figures rose steadily to 250 vehicles a year, giving BT the second highest vehicle sales in Blankshire.

I believe that my experience with a major Japanese motor company has given me an invaluable background in promoting the Japanese philosophy of quality control and repeat customers.

Whilst I should be very happy to be involved in Fleet Sales of Nissan vehicles, I now feel ready in my career to accept the major challenge of working for a large dealership with a franchise for a wider range of vehicles.

If you would like me to enlarge upon any of the above points, I should be happy to do so in an interview.

Yours sincerely

John Roberts

JOHN ROBERTS

Note: This letter indicates substantial experience as a sales executive, together with a year's experience in a related field of the motor trade. That he was **invited** to become a sales trainee indicates that others saw promise in him at an early age. That promise was fulfilled with the invitation to head Fleet Sales.

The candidate uses the term 'career' several times to indicate that he enjoys this work and does not regard it as a passing phase. He implies his own drive and enthusiasm; has experience of a thriving work environment; stresses the advantage he feels he has in understanding Japanese methods; and, above all, places great emphasis upon customer satisfaction. His main priority is to gain wider experience, but his co-ordination background may well place him in a position for a more senior sales post in the company.

Although the letter is very detailed, no paragraph is over nine lines long. This makes it easy on the eye.

SPECULATIVE LETTERS OF APPLICATION

A speculative letter is a letter written to an employer by someone expressing interest in working for that organisation, or enquiring whether there are any job vacancies.

Often, the writer may not specify the type of job — he has just always wanted to work for the BBC or British Airways etc. Alternatively, the writer may be particularly well qualified in a particular sphere, as a geophysicist for example, and is approaching all the oil exploration companies.

In times of high unemployment such as we are currently experiencing, this may seem a rather pointless exercise. But, in fact, it is often estimated that up to 30% of all job vacancies are never advertised publicly — the jobs go to friends or relatives of people already working in the organisation or to someone whom an employee can recommend. So, such 'speculation' might well pay off, if you are suited to that type of job.

Speculative letters tend to be more successful in the private sector which may have less formal application procedures than public bodies. But they can be particularly successful with people seeking a first job — the employer will be impressed by someone showing initiative.

Of course, the employer may have no vacancies but you can request that he keeps your name on file for any future vacancies which may occur.

The most favoured way to send a speculative letter is to send **three** documents:

a brief letter
a CV
a personal details sheet 'fleshing out' your CV.

The letter

Since you are not applying for a specific job, the letter can only be brief, outlining your interest.

The CV

Use a standard CV here.

The Personal Details Sheet

This needs particular care because it gives an overall impression of you, your background and qualifications, interests and abilities without the more personal approach necessary in a letter of application for a **specific** job. A well-written sheet, on **one** side of A4, could be used for a range of similar jobs.

Let us take the example of a graduate geophysicist who is writing speculative letters to all the major oil companies operating in the U.K.

Flat 2
46 Kensall Rise
Headingley
Leeds
LS12 8BM
12th August 199-

The Personnel Director
Conoco Ltd
Conoco House
230 Blackfriars Road
London SE1 6UP

Dear Sir

I enclose herewith my CV and personal details sheet.

I should be very grateful if you could inform me whether there are any current or forthcoming vacancies for geophysicists with your company.

I look forward to hearing from you soon.

Yours faithfully

Brendan O'Neill

BRENDAN O'NEILL

CURRICULUM VITAE

NAME:	Brendan O'Neill
ADDRESS:	Flat 2, 46 Kensall Rise, Headingley, Leeds LS12 8BM
TELEPHONE:	Work: 0532 667478 ext. 209 Home: 0532 427791
DATE OF BIRTH:	10.04.1963
AGE:	27
PLACE OF BIRTH:	Sunderland, Tyne and Wear
NATIONALITY:	British
MARITAL STATUS:	Single
EDUCATION:	St. Benedict's R.C. Grammar School, Sunderland 1975-1982 University of Leeds 1982-1985, 1985-86
QUALIFICATIONS:	A Level: Mathematics B, Physics B, Geology B } 1982 B.Sc. (Hons.) 1st Class, Mining Engineering, University of Leeds, 1985 M.Sc. Geophysics, University of Leeds, 1986
EXPERIENCE:	Research Assistant, Minerals and Data Research Unit, University of Leeds, 1986 to date. Includes laboratory and data analysis for oil, gas and mineral exploration. Fieldwork research/exploration conducted for: British Gas, Wytch Farm, Dorset 1987 British Coal, Long Eaton, Notts. 1988 Western Goldfields, California 1985-1986 Conoco/Amoco/Phillips contracts 1985-90
REFEREES:	Prof. D. Langer Dept. Earth Sciences University of Leeds Leeds LS99 1XX Dr. G. Cross Manager Minerals & Data Research Unit University of Leeds Leeds LS99 1XX
PERIOD OF NOTICE:	6 weeks

Brendan O'Neill

PERSONAL DETAILS SHEET

After gaining my degree in Mining Engineering (with First Class Honours), I undertook an M.Sc. in Geophysics, researching the Stratification of the Ryedale Valley.

Since completing my M.Sc. I have worked in the Minerals and Data Research Unit at Leeds University. The work has included extensive computer analysis of data supplied by major oil companies to the Unit, together with active fieldwork, prospecting for oil, coal and gold.

The extensive data analysis has been principally from multi-national oil companies like Conoco, Amoco and Phillips, who have wished to make full use of the facilities offered by Leeds University, as they do not themselves possess comprehensive laboratory facilities in the U.K. However, I have also completed additional contract work for Shell, BP and Esso. I am therefore accustomed to working to deadlines on both major long-term contract work and on short 'rush' jobs.

The fieldwork has given me the opportunity to prospect both by computer predictions and practically in the field in a variety of conditions above and below ground. This has given me wide experience of handling in reality the theoretical work done in the laboratory. As a result of my laboratory analysis for Western Goldfields, I was asked to lead the 3 months exploratory work for the company in California.

Although I have also worked on contracts for British Coal and British Gas, I have always found that my real interest is in the oil industry.

I now feel ready to extend my career working exclusively for a major oil company for which I have already done contract work, and to which I can bring my varied experience.

Note: The personal statement does not need signing — it is not a letter. Each paragraph should deal with a major new point.

A speculative letter will not necessarily bring results but is well worth trying, if your circumstances warrant it. Again, word processing the letter will save considerable time and effort.

If you are applying for your first job, you are unable to refer directly to permanent paid employment. This may of course be a disadvantage. But before you despair, ask yourself the following questions:

Have I had a . . .
. . . work experience programme in school or college?
. . . weekend job?
. . . holiday job?
. . . temporary job?
Have I helped parents or someone else in their job?
Have I done voluntary work for any organisation?
Have I been a member of a club, society or body which has allowed me to develop or use particular skills? (e.g. scouts/guides/sports where I may have developed leadership skills, handled money, used my own initiative.)

You may well find that you do have experience in one or more of these areas. If so, use it to your advantage.

Refer back to page 18 **now** and to the list you made for yourself. These are qualities you will want to bring out in a letter, particularly if you don't have direct employment experience.

SAMPLE LETTER FOR FIRST JOB

Let's take the example of Kim Lee who has seen the following job advertised and thinks it would be suitable:

> VACANCY
>
> Office junior for busy hotel complex. Experience not necessary as training will be given. Salary negotiable. Apply by letter to: Manager, Palm Hotel, Barton Promenade, Ramsey Island.

Kim's list of experience is limited because of having no paid employment.

It reads: 4 modest GCSEs — English, Maths, Geography, Commerce.
Occasional help with family taxi hire business (answering the telephone, taking bookings).
Hobbies: home computing, cooking, discos.

This is how Kim might use this limited experience in a letter of application for the above job.

18 Ocean Heights
Perth Street
Ramsey Island
14 June 199-

The Manager
Palm Hotel
Barton Promenade
Ramsey Island

Dear Sir/Madam

I would like to apply for the post of office junior, advertised in yesterday's 'Ramsey Echo'.

I have recently left Byron School with GCSE passes in English, Maths, Geography and Commerce. As all these subjects involved 80% coursework, I know already that I have achieved a pass standard at least, and am awaiting the examination board's confirmation of these grades next month.

The subjects studied are all relevant to the office junior post advertised. I particularly enjoyed Maths and gained experience of some basic accounts in the final term. As all the subjects were examined by a substantial amount of coursework, I have had experience over the last two years in meeting deadlines and of spreading my workload. I think that this is a very useful experience for clerical work.

I have had some experience of helping with the family taxi business. Answering the phone and taking bookings have given me confidence in dealing with the customer directly and in telephone technique.

I am interested in home computing and cooking, which I think are interests that would be helpful in the hotel business. My interest in disco dancing would allow me to recommend appropriate discos in the area for the hotel's information leaflets to guests.

I hope that you will be able to consider me for the advertised job.

I look forward to hearing from you.

Yours faithfully

Kim Lee

Important points from the letter:

It:

* is polite
* concentrates on the positives by omitting reference to ‘modest’ passes or to any failures
* ties in Kim’s limited experience to the demands of the job
* emphasises Kim’s experience by **using** the word several times.

Even if you feel that you have **no** suitable work experience, tie in your hobbies, background and lifestyle with the job to make the most of yourself.

SUMMARY

We have now gone through the four essential steps towards gaining a job interview. You will have seen that, depending on the job and what you are asked to submit, a good overall application is a matter of carefully selecting and balancing material, and then presenting it in a polished manner.

Let us summarise the advantages and disadvantages of the various components.

APPLICATION FORM	Employer:	Presents essential information in desired sequence. Express him/herself.	Does not allow applicant to organise and edit material or express him/herself.
	Applicant:	Neat form will stand out from mediocre.	Ditto
CURRICULUM VITAE	Employer:	Gives at-a-glance summary — useful reminder in interview.	Allows organisation and editing but little self-expression.
	Applicant:	Can 'highlight' strengths.	Poorly prepared CV will eliminate any chance you have.
LETTER	Employer:	Allows assessment of candidates' written fluency.	No set order to information. Poor letter difficult to summarise.
	Applicant:	Can 'tailor' material to specific job vacancy.	Weak letter will give very poor impression.

Each part of the application performs a different function but they all complement each other.

The key words here are **selection** and **balance**, together with **neat presentation**.

CURRICULUM VITAE

NAME:

ADDRESS:

TELEPHONE:

DATE OF BIRTH:

PLACE OF BIRTH:

NATIONALITY:

MARITAL STATUS:

EDUCATION:

QUALIFICATIONS:

EXPERIENCE:

REFERENCES:

PERIOD OF NOTICE:

Part I has taken you step by step through the application process. I hope that it has given you the self-confidence to prepare a really good application for a job.

Good luck.

PART TWO

PREPARING FOR AN INTERVIEW

The amount of notice you will receive for an interview may vary from several days to a month or so. There are many useful preparations you can make during this time.

Background Information

It is helpful to do some research about the organisation, as well as the specific job, in the time leading up to the interview. I know of a young lady who had an interview for a Saturday Sales Assistant's post at Mothercare: she was amazed when she was asked what she knew about the company. So don't assume because the job you're applying for is not an 'executive' or 'managerial' one, that ignorance is permissible.

Here are some questions which could be applicable to a wide variety of organisations such as:

Is it a large or small firm?
Is it in the public or private sector?
If it is quoted on the Stock Exchange, is the share price increasing or decreasing?
Is it part of a group?
Where are its headquarters?
Approximately how many people are employed?
What is its annual turnover?
Is it a growing or contracting industry?
Do its employees belong to a union? If so, which one(s)?
Has it a good industrial relations record?
Who is its Chief Executive and/or Managing Director?
Has it been in the news lately? If so, why?
Have any recent economic or political events been likely to affect it?

Where To Find the Information (applicable to larger companies only)

You may have been sent some information when you first applied. If not, a letter to the Public Relations Officer requesting pamphlets etc. about the firm's products, and, with a public company, a copy of the annual report to shareholders, could provide you with much useful information.

The Reference Section of most public libraries should also be of help. For example, 'Who Owns Whom' may be appropriate to your needs.

The business sections of newspapers can also be useful. Remember that you don't have to buy them — just visit the reading room of your local library.

Keep abreast of the news in the days/weeks leading up to your interview. Topical events may well have an effect on a company's trade, or industrial relations.

Last, but by no means least, ask relatives, friends and acquaintances what **they** know of the firm, remembering that their opinion will be highly personal.

Likely Questions You May Be Asked

The fact that you have been invited for interview means that your experience and/or qualifications, and references, have favourably impressed your interviewer. He or she will now be interested in you as a person. To some of the questions he asks, he will be interested not so much in **what** you answer but **how** you answer.

Many people, quite understandably, are nervous and embarrassed at answering 'personal' questions but it is vitally important to anticipate some of these, to think carefully about your response and to jot down some 'practice replies'.

A useful exercise, which can then be used as the basis for a number of answers, is to make a list of your strengths and weaknesses. Do this honestly: don't underplay your strengths, but don't ignore your faults either.

When you are asked, as is very likely, 'Why should we choose **you** out of our many applicants for this job?', you will then be able to draw upon those qualities you've already thought about and listed, which seemed most appropriate for the job. For example:

A prospective primary school teacher may wish to stress her patience; her calm, unruffled temperament; and her sense of humour.

A prospective sales representative might stress his or her persuasiveness, determination, and ability to communicate clearly with a wide variety of people.

You might be asked, in addition to the above, 'What faults do you have which might make you unsuitable for the job?' Your immediate response might be to answer, 'None at all', but this could well come over as arrogance. It would be better to mention a 'minor' weakness which would not adversely affect your chances. A nurse might say, 'I suppose at first I might be in danger of being too emotionally involved in the future of my patients, but I'm sure I would soon manage to strike the right balance between compassion and professional detachment.'

Below is a list of awkward questions which have been asked in an interview. Don't worry! Very few interviewers will ask questions as bluntly as these unless you are applying for a very high-powered job. It is useful, however, to think about them carefully and note down your answers so that you can refer to them whenever the occasion demands.

1. Describe yourself in 3 adjectives.

To make this slightly easier, I've listed several. Are any appropriate to you? Which others would you add?

creative	adventurous
sensitive	thorough
organised	eccentric
dynamic	extrovert
patient	gregarious
assertive	methodical
compassionate	persuasive
generous	polite
competitive	quick-thinking
ambitious	loyal
determined	flexible

Note: In this instance you would want to describe yourself in the most positive light. Hence 'determined' rather than 'stubborn', 'thorough' rather than 'plodding' should be used.

2. What is your proudest achievement?

Remember that this need not relate to academic achievement at all. Be honest. It could be anything from learning to swim at age 30, after being terrified of water all your life; giving birth to your first baby; negotiating a truce between your rebellious teenage son and his grandmother. This type of answer also applies to points 6 and 7.

3. Are you too young/old for the job?

If you are young, stress enthusiasm, fresh outlook, stamina — tempered with willingness to learn from senior, experienced colleagues. If you are older, stress value of experience, broad knowledge, 'mature' outlook but also willingness to learn new approaches and to adapt. In other words, try to project yourself as a **balanced** person where age is, perhaps, immaterial.

4. Are you an aggressive person?

If the job requires some degree of aggression, it may be better to say that you are ***assertive***.

5. Do you often lose your temper? Why?

Again, it will not necessarily be looked upon as a fault to admit that you **occasionally** lose your temper, if the reason is justifiable. Anger at witnessing obvious injustice is more excusable than losing your temper because a subordinate hasn't understood a task you've asked him to complete. (This is an answer which requires great care.)

6. What's the best idea you've had in the last year?

7. What's the hardest thing you've done in the last three years?

8. What would you like to be doing in five years'/ten years' time?

Some people will have very definite aims in terms of career progression. This can be most commendable, but avoid the over-threatening 'I'd like to be in your chair doing your job,' even if you **do** harbour that wish! If you haven't any clear picture of what you want to do, you could say something like — 'For the immediate future I shall enjoy the challenge of learning and perfecting the skills which this job will provide. I may find that I want to develop one particular aspect of the job later on, but I'm keeping my options open at the moment'.

9. Which is more important to you: money or status?

A potentially embarrassing question for some people perhaps. You may like to consider the following ideas: To be comfortable financially is desirable; it enables you and your family to pursue a certain lifestyle. Status implies responsibility, the idea that you will have earned the respect of others brings personal satisfaction in that you will have achieved some of your aims/ambitions.

10. Tell me about yourself.

If you've done the earlier exercise and thought carefully about those previous questions, you will have a much clearer idea of how to answer this very generalised question.

11. Why do you want to leave your present job?

If the job you are applying for implies a promotion, the interviewer will naturally understand your motives — you can say 'I'm looking for greater responsibility and challenge than my current job offers and I believe that the job advertised will offer these.'

If the job is a sideways move, or a move into an entirely different sphere of work, the interviewer may be more searching about your motives. (But don't forget that the very fact that you *are* being interviewed means that the employer considers you a definite possibility.) In such circumstances, it is crucial that you

* avoid sounding negative or critical of your present employer.
* don't make it sound as if it is **you** who is difficult to get along with.

There may be other positive factors about the new job that you would want to stress:

* The job is significantly nearer home
* You are aware of the good reputation or excellent career opportunities of the prospective employer.

The importance of advance preparation of these questions cannot be overstressed.

Questions You May Wish To Ask

It is important to make a note of any questions you may wish to ask, even though, during the course of the interview you may find that many, if not all, are answered for you.

Such questions may include wanting to clarify your specific responsibilities, working conditions, your opportunities for further training, promotion prospects, pension provision, holiday entitlement and pay. It is important **not** to seem as if the latter two points are **all** you are interested in.

Do make sure that you are not asking about something which has already been stated in the job advertisement, or in the printed information you've previously received.

The interviewer(s) will always give you the opportunity to ask questions. If all your queries have been answered fully and you really can't think of anything else to ask, then don't just confine yourself to a curt 'No'. Say something like, 'Thank you, but you seem to have covered very fully all the questions I had prepared.'

Documentation

Ensure that you have collected, in a neat folder, any documentation, i.e. certificates etc. which has been requested. This can then be placed on the floor beside your chair. You certainly want to avoid scrabbling in a handbag or jacket pocket for the requisite bits of paper!

Appearance

However unfair we may feel it to be, first impressions **do** count. Appearance is merely one facet of the 'whole' person that we want to project at the interview, but remember, your interviewer will **see** you before you begin **talking**, so it is wise to consider carefully your choice of dress for the occasion. A general rule would be: **look smart but comfortable**. You have many important things to think about at an interview: the last thing you want to be concerned about is tight-fitting shoes or hair that keeps falling into your eyes. Though there are obvious exceptions, you don't usually want to look too flamboyant. Be on the conservative side in your dress. If you are inclined to fiddle, avoid any jewellery with which you might be tempted to fiddle.

Timing

It may sound obvious, but arriving late for the interview will not create a good impression. Aim to arrive about **ten minutes early**.

You may need to consider all or some of the following points:

Do you have to travel far to the interview? Will you be going by (a) public transport, or (b) driving yourself?

If (a), ensure that you have consulted an up-to-date timetable and given yourself plenty of time to get from the station/bus-stop to the building where the interview is being held.

If (b), will there be parking facilities nearby? Is it practicable to have a 'dummy-run' if you are unsure of the area?

Many organisations will provide a map, even if it is only an 'internal' one of a large office or factory complex. Make sure you have it with you and know the appropriate name/title of your interviewer, in case you need to announce your arrival to a porter/receptionist.

It is better to be on the safe side and be early, rather than arrive flushed and breathless. This will also give you the opportunity to take a few deep breaths to relax yourself. If unforeseen circumstances do arise and you are late — **don't panic**. Apologise but make it clear that it was out of your control, then put this set-back out of your mind and concentrate on the interview.

Re-reading Your Application Form

Those of you who have read Part I will, of course, have made photocopies of your completed application form and/or letter and cv.

Re-read them as you prepare for your interview to remind yourself what information the interviewer(s) will have in front of them about you. It will also refresh your memory about the reasons you have given for wanting the job.

If you take all the necessary preparatory steps, you should arrive at the interview feeling more confident and relaxed, and ready to handle any potentially 'tricky' questions without being rendered speechless with surprise.

AT THE INTERVIEW

Before The Interview Proper

Depending on the type of job you are being interviewed for, and/or the custom of the employer, you will either be interviewed completely on your own, or as part of a small group of say, four to six candidates, each having an individual interview scheduled for a particular time of the day.

You'll probably be able to tell which format is used from the letter of invitation. Certainly, if a half-day or a day's timetable is drawn up, assume that other candidates will be there.

If you are the only candidate, you may well be interviewed just by one person at the appointed time. You'll probably be asked to wait outside a room or the interviewer's office, and then be shown in. If you need to, you can relax by taking a few deep breaths while you are waiting.

If you are one of a group, you'll probably all be shown into one room and supplied with a cup of coffee until all the candidates have arrived. When all the interviewees are gathered together without a host, some rather stilted conversation about the weather or the journey will emerge. That's fine — it breaks the ice and you're probably going to be in one anothers' company for some hours, so you may as well get on together. But **remember:** you're all going for the same job — **you are competitors**. So don't give away any of **your** reasons for wanting this job: your strengths, your weaknesses etc. Other candidates may actually use it **against** you in the interview. Be discreet with the other candidates throughout the day.

The Grand Tour

It is a normal practice to show a group of interview candidates around the workplace once they have all assembled. You may have one or several guides, who may form part of the interviewing panel or selection committee etc. ***Remember his or her name and designation*** e.g. John Brown, sales director; Peter Smith, plant manager; Jean Thompson, deputy headmistress. Use that person's name when you address him or her — people like to be called by their names.

Whilst on the tour, an informal interviewing process will be taking place — people will be summing you up: both the guide(s) and the other candidates. You need to show yourself to be interested and informed, but without seeming to be either a 'creep' or a show-off. A careful balance has to be achieved here — try to phrase questions which show both your **knowledge and your desire for information.**

Examples

> 'When you switched over to computerised stock-ordering, did you have any problems with customer reaction?'
>
> 'You introduced continuous-feed-unloaders 12 months ago. Did this present any problems with operators used to a two-shift system?'

I understand that you have a CPVE course in Hospitality. How do you select students for this course?

Note that in each of these cases, the statement comes first, followed by the question, indicating to the listener prior knowledge followed by an information-seeking question.

Avoid making many comments during your tour unless they are directly on what is being shown and are genuinely favourable. General comments can give the wrong impression. You may have been to interviews before where you have assessed from the comments made, which of the other candidates is **not** going to get the job. The guide is doing the same, so the main advice at this stage is to **keep your own counsel**.

The other purpose of the tour is to allow you to assess whether you want to work in this establishment. All interviews are a two-way affair and you are free to withdraw your application or even turn down a job offer if you think that the job, the company or the personnel is not right for you.

THE INTERVIEW PROPER

Whether you have a tour or not, the most important part of the day is the interview proper. You will be invited into a room with an interviewer or a panel of interviewers. For many of the panel, or indeed the lone interviewer, this is the first time that they will see you. So remember, **first impressions count**.

Adopt the following procedure:

Entry

If you need to knock on the door, do so positively and confidently.

Enter in a brisk, confident manner.

Smile and say 'Good morning' or 'Good afternoon' but don't grin.

Shake hands firmly if a hand is proffered. (Don't go and shake everybody by the hand if no-one offers to shake yours.)

Wait to be invited to sit down.

Sit in an upright position, don't slouch. Put your handbag or document case on the floor at the side of your chair.

Listen to everyone's name as they are being introduced, and remember them if there are no nameplates. (You may need to memorise them by some sort of mnemonic pattern. E.g. Mrs **Wright** is on the **right**, Mr **Davis** is by the **door**, Mr **Gresham** is in a **green** jacket. It may not be as easy as this, but try somehow to remember them.)

Make Sure You Are Comfortable

If the sun is in your eyes, ask politely if you can move your chair or if a blind can be drawn.

Be Positive About the Interview

You wouldn't be there if you didn't stand a reasonable chance.

Suppress Visible Nervous Behaviour

As previously mentioned, interview nerves are natural. Interviewers themselves are also nervous and have to be (or should be) trained in controlling them. There are a number of ways you can get on top of your nerves, and **correct posture is the key**.

Sitting in a cross-legged position (men) or a cross-ankled position (women) in an armless chair will:

* help you sit upright without looking 'starchy'.
* keep your hands still in your lap.
* allow any hand gestures you make seem more restrained and natural.
* prevent you biting your nails.
* allow better eye contact.

Even if you are sitting in a chair with arms it is better to keep your hands in your lap.

A Natural Tone Of Voice

A tense, high-pitched voice, a loud voice, an aggressive tone, very quiet speech or a delivery that is too fast or too slow all create a poor impression. You need to speak loudly enough to be heard clearly, sound confident but not aggressive, have a natural tone of voice, and deliver at a comfortable pace.

Smoking

Don't smoke unless invited to do so, and even then, try not to unless absolutely necessary.

Fidgeting

If you're a fidgeter, avoid wearing necklaces which you'll be fiddling with, and don't twiddle rings or cuff-links.

Maintain Good Eye Contact

Look the interviewer in the eye confidently without adopting a transfixing stare. If there are several interviewers, look at them equally in turn — you'll make them all feel involved with the interview process, and impress them all instead of just the one directly in front of you.

Refer To Any Documentation Required From Your Neatly Arranged Document File

Pauses

Interviewers are trained to expect a slight pause whilst the interviewee 'frames' his or her answer. Make use of this time and don't rush into replying — this is when you may say something you'll regret.

You can always use the **occasional** delaying tactic:
'That depends upon how you interpret X. I'm inclined to think that . . .' Or, 'It's perfectly natural that you should raise that point.' These are devices which allow you to speak without committing yourself, whilst still working out your answer. Watch politicians do it all the time!

Making Notes

You may wish to make notes about things said or asked in the interview. Ask if it is alright to do so. The employer realises that an interview is not a memory test but, even so, make notes discreetly and sparingly.

Expand Upon The Questions Asked

Don't give a simple 'Yes' or 'No', even if the interviewer asks a poorly phrased question. The interviewer(s) will be looking for you to develop the issues raised in questions.

Use Appropriate Language

Avoid slang and casual language: Be precise and formal in your response. For example, say: 'Yes, I would certainly enjoy that' rather than, 'Yeah, that would be magic.' Avoid meaningless phrases like '. . . sort of . . .', '. . . kind of . . .', '. . . you know . . .', '. . . like . . .', etc.

Use the same terminology as the interviewer(s). If he talks consistently of 'sales executives' rather than 'salesmen', do the same; if he talks of 'human resources', use that term rather than 'personnel'.

Listen

Listen carefully to what is said. Don't answer a question you would like to have been asked instead of one which was actually asked.

Assess whether the interviewers are using 'buzz' words, displaying their particular concerns or interests. Try to capitalise on these.

Listen also to the way the interviewer phrases a question. He may ask: 'Which do you think is more important: Marketing itself, or Research and Development, where you also have the opportunity to develop products suited to your market?' You receive a clear hint here that the questioner attaches more importance to the second point. Of course, making a decision between two concepts may be difficult and they may not be mutually exclusive anyway. But listening carefully to the phrasing of the questions will give you a clear indication of the desired response.

Ask Questions As Well As Answer Them

As previously mentioned, this shows that you are prepared, thoughtful and realistic.

Be Yourself

It's no use trying to put on an act or to pretend to be a different personality. You won't be able to sustain it.

Conclude The Interview Positively

Ensure that everything you want to cover has been covered. Don't leave with any misunderstandings about duties, contract, etc.

Exit Positively

Thank the interviewers with a smile for their time, shake hands if appropriate, and leave the room in a positive, confident way. (Tip: When you enter the room, remember where the door is. Don't head off in the wrong direction!)

WAITING YOUR TURN

Where there are a number of candidates, waiting your turn for the interview can be the most nerve-racking time. Candidates are often interviewed in alphabetical order of surname, but don't get caught out if there is a different procedure. In any case, the organisation should tell you the running order and approximate length of the interview. (That time will pass very quickly when you are actually being interviewed.)

Those of you who have attended 'group' interviews will probably have experienced the anguish of another candidate being out of the room for 20-30 minutes, returning in a jovial mood, cracking jokes and generally behaving in an insensitive way towards those still steeling themselves. Likewise, the interviewee who returns, depressed at his own dismal performance and at how unfair the questions were, can infect those still waiting.

All you can do is to ignore these two reactions: don't get drawn into them. At the same time, listen for any useful clues the previous interviewees might drop: the interviewer on the right likes intellectual responses; the one on the left doesn't like you to stare at him, etc.

Go prepared for a long wait. Take a note-pad to jot down any **last-minute** ideas that come to you; take a book of crossword puzzles, a newspaper or something that will keep you mentally alert without distracting you from your main purpose.

AFTER THE INTERVIEW

Either you will be told on the spot whether you've got the job or you'll be informed by post later.

If you get the job — great! You won't need to read this manual until your next job interview!

If not, go home, relax and be positive. Don't grieve over the lost opportunity but assess your performance as dispassionately as you can. Was there any particular area of experience which let you down, so that you can try to rectify that before applying for another similar job? Was there any question which caught you out? Or any response you made which you thought was less than convincing? How can you work on this? **Accept the interview for the positive experience it is**.

If you will not know the outcome for several weeks, it would be unwise to convince yourself one way or the other about the outcome. Again, you can reflect upon the experience — you will have some intuition about what went well or badly.

CLAIMING EXPENSES

Don't forget that the majority of organisations will allow you to claim expenses for attending the interview, although the successful candidate may not receive them until after he or she has taken up the appointment.

Some organisations, like the Civil Service and a number of major companies, will pay you on the spot in cash, so have your expenses sheet ready with an estimate of any extra expenses incurred on the return trip, besides the fare or mileage. (E.g. meals, hotel bills etc.)

Otherwise, you'll submit the claim with appropriate receipts, when you return home. Don't forget to check all that you can include, and what you are prohibited from claiming. If you are claiming from a Local Authority, don't be surprised if they don't re-imburse you for several months. Being interviewed for several teaching jobs, for example, in different parts of the country, could prove to be an expensive business, particularly if it is your first job. A photocopy of the expenses claim(s) should assist your bank manager in deciding whether a loan or overdraft is in order.

Remember also that some employers, particularly for executive recruitment in the private sector, will quite happily pay relocation expenses. These may include all or some of the following: estate agents' fees, legal fees, removal costs, bridging loan, 'disturbance' allowance. Check exactly what is or is not covered before committing yourself to the job. No employer is going to offer this for fun, he may have to do it to attract candidates of the right calibre to a particular geographical area. Don't find yourself caught out and financially worse off because of a misunderstanding.

RECRUITMENT AGENCY INTERVIEWS

Sometimes you may be interviewed for a job by an agency — a specialist recruitment agency in the private sector like Blue Arrow, PER (the Professional and Executive Recruitment division of the Manpower Services Commission), or by a Jobcentre.

If this is so, there may be a representative of the employing organisation present, or the agency may have been given complete discretion in the selection of staff (having been given a precise brief by the employer). Certainly, you will be dealing with professional interviewers who may be less tolerant of lapses or shortcomings in interview, but their training should make the interview a stimulating and valuable experience for you.

If you are to be interviewed by an agency, all the information provided in this package will still apply.

You may find that some agencies will charge a fee direct to the prospective job-hunter. This is unusual in Britain, but in some other countries e.g. Singapore, it is quite common. It might also apply if you are considering a job with a company **based** in another country.

When you first approach an agency

* clarify at the outset whether you will be charged a fee.
* under what circumstances a fee is payable.
* how much it will be.

You don't want an unpleasant shock at a later stage.

If it seems a common practice in your area to pay a fee, find out from other people who may have used agencies how they rate them. In such circumstances, personal recommendation of an agency is the best yardstick.

INTERVIEWS BY TELEPHONE

There are very few jobs where the appointment is made solely by telephone interview, and then only if the candidate is known personally or by reputation, to the employer.

The initial request for job information may have been by telephone, and some financial organisations (like life assurance companies, insurance or commodity brokers) may ask you to telephone them and explain why you think you are suited to the job. This is because you would do a lot of selling or making contacts by phone, and they are testing your telephone technique. But such initial approaches, if successful, would always be followed up by a formal face-to-face interview.

Any interview, or pre-interview session, which involves the medium of the telephone must require you to think carefully in advance whether you are temperamentally suited to this technique. If you think you are, read a book on telephone sales techniques from your local library.

PRACTICE INTERVIEWS

You can easily practise at home how you are going to complete an application form or letter. You can also get someone who knows you well to check over what you have written and suggest any amendments before you write the final version. You cannot do the same with interviews.

There is no substitute for experience with interviews, which makes it particularly difficult for those facing their first one. You can gain some useful experience from anyone in a supervisory or management position above you in work, if they are willing to conduct a mock interview with you. Annual appraisal interviews can also provide you with useful experience. If you do work for a very large organisation with a well-organised training or personnel department, interview skills may well feature in their training programme. These can be extremely useful, particularly if there is a video facility so that you can watch your own posture, mannerisms etc. It's not as frightening as it sounds!

For those who are unemployed, your local Jobcentre, PER office or Job Training Scheme may be able to offer some advice or practice.

But it is extremely difficult to prepare yourself mentally and to get the adrenalin flowing for a mock job in which you have no **real** interest. It is also totally unprofitable to have a role-play interview with a friend or relative as practice for a real interview the next day. **It simply will not work**. Either you'll become flustered and embarrassed, which will depress you, or you'll be given such an easy ride that you won't prepare yourself properly for the real thing.

CONCLUSION

You should now have all the information on hand to enable you to make a good impression at the interview.

Remember that the first lesson about approaching any interview is to **BE POSITIVE**.

The second lesson is to **BE YOURSELF**.